MW00975722

Oops I Hit a Bump On the Road!

5 Motivating Chapters to Help You Get Back On Track..

Printed in the USA ISBN:9781727469912

Dedication

To all my New Yorkers! We got through 9/11 with fears , tears and pain - but we did not let anything stop us from purpose and during this pandemic we will continue to press through. To every Bride that has had to cancel her wedding, Every graduate who was unable to have their prom and graduation day ,   every person who has experienced loss and fears. To those who think it's over for them, for the small business owner , running your office from home - this book is for you.

Think BIG and Be intentional.

Besos y Hugs,
Genie Santos

Introduction

Hi there Friend. Thank you for picking up this book. In this book you will find some very relatable moments. After writing 7 faith based inspirational and informational books I decided to write one that everyone in the general public would like to read. We may not all have the same faith in common and each person may believe in a higher power differently than I do. But, one thing is for sure and that is that we all have hit a bumpy road at some point in life and that we all have in common. So, You just hit a bump on the road and you look a mess. Get your hair out your eyes, that's if you have any hair. Hey bald is cool too. Straighten up your clothes. Pick up everything you dropped and let's get it together.

Follow me to the pages of this book,

Table of Content

Chapter 1:

Everything Seemed aligned then KATAPOOM!

When I first began to write this book, I was flowing naturally. I began to write it in 2018 and everything was falling into place then KATAPOOM!. I had stopped at chapter 3 and was handling some texts that were coming in; I noticed I must've hit something and erased everything. So, if you think you're the only one who hits the bumps on the road you're mistaken. I invite you to sit down and relax. Yikes! Some of you have a tired face. Drink some water and just read on. We often plan for things and we get excited especially when we're going to do something or start something that means a lot to us. However, oftentimes we find that things don't turn out the way we plan.

I had planned my whole entire life in my late twenties and no I'm not living in Virginia , I don't own a pug , not married to that person anymore and my kids are not away in college. Life happened to me in more ways than one and for a while I was in a rut. Came out one rut to find a new challenge. But I had to make the best of each moment and choose to view my mountains close up by climbing over them instead of standing below looking up and contemplating on their height!

Even now as I find myself finally rewriting this book it seems like the whole world hit a big bump on the road. This year started with Fires in Australia, Earthquakes in Puerto Rico, Pandemic worldwide, Locust in Africa, Murder Hornets and

Gypsy moths in Washington State. Can somebody say JUMANJI?

Weddings canceled, sweet sixteen canceled, Virtual baby showers - quarantined - social distance and many working from home or not working at all.

Talk about a bump on the road. Everyone's plans just completely shifted unexpectedly.

A booming economy has gone spiraling down. But in all this mayhem going on around the world and in our own backyards.(By the way, I don't own a backyard, it just sounds nice) We must be able to climb the mountains, swim across oceans and still sing "Don't worry, be happy."

It is easier said than done. Some things have fallen apart because of wrong timing, wrong decisions or just plain old circumstances that are out of our control. Discouragement, fear of the unknown and a changing world in front of us should not keep us from accomplishing the purposes in our lives.

Chapter 2:

Overcoming Yourself

Did you know that even at a time like this, you are the only one who can stop where you are going? Let me explain. Yes everything you had laid out on the table has had some interference. Seems like a major interruption has taken place in your life. But I find that oftentimes even when changes happen they play a purpose in my circumstance. It has had to be left up to me to get up and push forward. Yes, perhaps the plan has to be rerouted, delayed or changed. It does not mean that's an excuse for me to sit around and cry over it and not try to figure out what's next. I know it can be so hard at times. I am a very determined woman. When I say I am going to do something I do it. Yep, you bet your NIKE I just do it! However, there have been moments where the circumstance, the unexpected change has intimidated my very being. Those are the times I have to look in the mirror and talk to that lady and remind her of all the other obstacle courses she has come through. Yeah there's been some bumps and bruises but what did not kill me made me stronger. What did I learn? Well, I have learned that in order to cross the river I have to overcome myself. I have to overcome my unanswered questions. I have to really believe that my passions are in my heart for a reason and that what I am fighting for will not only benefit me but others around me as well. Therefore the world can be on shutdown but that does not mean my dreams are on shut down, my planning, my future. The biggest obstacle you have is not the pandemic or the government the biggest obstacle is not a murder hornet, the biggest obstacle is you.

When you are born for greatness you have to believe you have what it takes even if life has served you a different plate of breakfast.

Write down your 5 strongest qualities below:

_____

_____

_____

_____

_____

I want you to understand that those qualities you just wrote are the same weapons you pick up and use to fight the whimpering, doubtful , fearful you. There is no failed plan A that cannot be overcome by a Plan B, C, D, please don't make me go through the alphabet here. World events, painful breakups, broken homes, race, disappointments of life in general do not dictate who you are and where you are going. Only you can!

Chapter 3:

Crossing the Bridge With Your Shoes off

On September 11, 2001, my wonderful city of NY experienced a shaking. Many lives and dreams were shattered on that Monday morning. I could never forget that day and the days thereafter. I had the opportunity to be involved in the relief efforts along with my church and met many people from many walks of life. Met many devastated wives, dads and so forth as they would stop by our prayer table before they went into St. Vincent's Medical Center to identify the remains of what could be their loved ones. That day of 9/11 many were stuck in the city and other boroughs. All transportation came to a halt. Their plans for that day and the days, months and years to come were completely unexpectedly changed. Many folks had to return home and cross our bridges. Some walked for hours in the midst of fears of terrorism. They might have crossed those bridges saying a prayer, some maybe drinking tears, and others just longing to come back home to their loved ones. Whichever the case was they did not stay put. The people began to head to their destinations. They were the remaining alive and though it was awfully painful they had to get home. Some might have had to take off their shoes in order to cross the bridge. That's where I now want to take you. You might be at the most important crossroad of your life right now. You have come a long way and all of a sudden in your journey you came across a bad experience. Perhaps, you are so tired your feet hurt from the journey and though your success is right across that bridge you are terrorized by what's behind you. You are intimidated by all the negative noise going on in your head. But dear, you must cross that bridge even if your feet hurt and you're afraid of heights. TAKE OFF YOUR SHOES if you must and cross it. Yes you might have to cross it without that person who was in your life, maybe you have to move from where you are at to a new place. You must not pay attention to the hurting calluses on your feet and take off the shoes and CROSS OVER to your home, your destination and your purpose.

Chapter 4:

Reinventing Yourself

My sweetheart is always quoting Benjamin Franklin, "If you fail to plan, you are planning to fail". That is so very true especially in this day and age. Maybe your biggest monkey wrench in the system is that you are feeling you are old school. You were one time the wonder boy or wonder girl of your company, but everything has evolved and you can't seem to be able to be on top again like you were before. We have seen many businesses just go out of business especially in retail. Why is that? Because in a world that is constantly evolving with the times there are just some things you cannot keep doing the same because it won't work the same. Maybe your struggle is that you moved away and started a new job elsewhere and they don't do things the way you are used to. Oh yes that can be so nerve wrecking. We get so used to a routine, a way of doing things and become so comfortable with it we go in total shock when the change comes. Even as I am writing this current pandemic has caused such havoc not only taking lives but altering lifestyles, habits and changing plans. One example is the churches. I am a Pastor myself and I have had to reinvent the ministry. That word has been in my head for a long time REINVENT almost as if something was telling me change was coming. I cannot sit down and cry over not having a building or a gathering with the congregants, but I sure can look within me and find all sorts of creativity and new ways to make our worship time happen. This is true for anything you have your heart on. Maybe there has to be a change. Reinvent yourself, don't put yourself in a box and call it quits. You're working from home? There are so many platforms on social media that can help you push forward. Yes you may have to tweak some things, remove some things, add some new things but in reinventing yourself you're going to find out there is more to you than you can ever imagine. Perhaps your divorce or financial situation has made you down. Hey it could be worse, you have the power to make things happen it's all in what you set your mind and heart to do and if reinventing yourself is necessary then put out the old and embrace the new. There is a verse in the good book that says you cannot put new wine into old wineskins ponder on that for a moment.

Chapter 5:

Be Intentional

I have learned through many situations in my life that giving up was not an option. Many times I have failed at many things I have set out to do and many times things that were blooming just fell apart because of unexpected scenarios created by others around me.

I finally arrived at a place of believing that I will not know how great I am at something if I don't give it a chance. So, I decided to Be intentional in all I set my heart to do. If the passion is there I'm going to intentionally pursue it, I'm going to intentionally try it. I may not have the money I need for a project but I'm going to act like I have the money and plan and move forward. I may not yet have my #1 best seller but I'm going to get up and continue writing books as if each one is the best seller. What are your goals? Are they a passing phase or is this your passion? Who said you're too old to learn to play the violin? Who says you cannot become the CEO of a company? Stop treating your home business as if it's just that, at home. Treat it as it's a big corporation, make your business cards the best, and make your ads on social media sound like you're serving millions of people. Be intentional towards your goal. Treat your little room like you're living in a mansion, paint it, decorate it Be intentional! Have a job interview dress for success, walk in there like you own it and if you don't get the job know there's a better door and that was just practice. Get over your failures, stop the pity party, we are not going to blow up your balloons - Be intentional with your life, your dreams, your hopes and your future.

Mirror Mirror on the wall, Who can overcome the bumps on the road?
You can! You have all it takes within you so go climb the mountain, overcome yourself, reinvent yourself and be intentional about it!

Fill in the blank.

Now Moving Forward :

I shall _____

I will _____

*I am*_____

I can _____

Notes

Notes

To invite Genie Santos to speak at your next event just email *Goodradiostation@gmail.com*

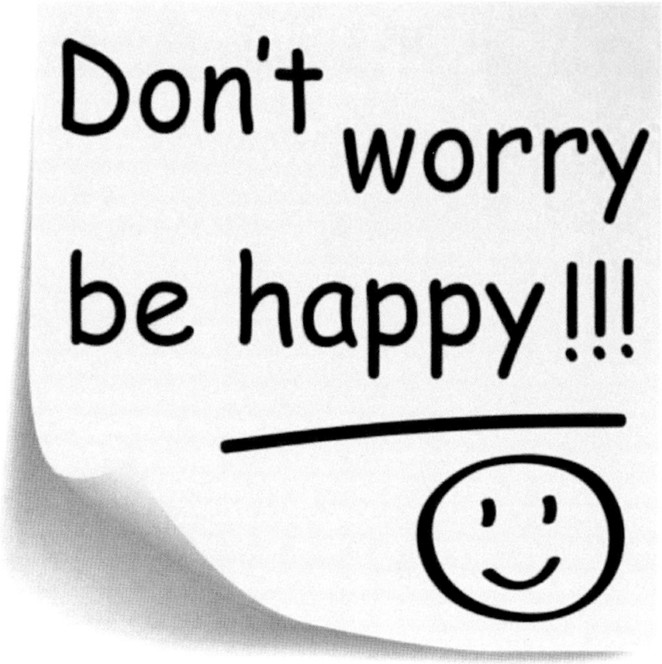
Don't worry
be happy!!!

"We are mountain movers, not mountain viewers!"
Pastor Genie Santos

Live on purpose and you'll find your purpose for living! Pastor Genie Santos

Made in the USA
Columbia, SC
13 October 2021

46892072R00015